A Gift for

From

Date

Your Great Name

written by Michael Neale and Krissy Nordhoff

Lost are saved; find their way; at the sound of Your great name.
All condemned; feel no shame; at the sound of Your great name.
Every fear; has no place; at the sound of Your great name.
The Enemy; he has to leave; at the sound of Your great name.

Jesus, Worthy is the Lamb that was slain for us, Son of God and Man
You are high and lifted up; that all the world will praise Your great name.

All the weak; find their strength; at the sound of Your great name.
Hungry souls; receive grace; at the sound of Your great name.
The fatherless; they find their rest; at the sound of Your great name.
Sick are healed; and the dead are raised; at the sound of Your great name.

Jesus, Worthy is the Lamb that was slain for us, Son of God and Man
You are high and lifted up; that all the world will praise Your great name.

YOUR GREAT NAME

DISCOVERING POWER *for* YOUR LIFE IN THE AWESOME NAMES *of* GOD

MICHAEL NEALE

summerside PRESS

Summerside Press™
Minneapolis, MN 55378
SummersidePress.com

Your Great Name
Discovering Power for Your Life in the Awesome Names of God

ISBN 978-1-60936-542-4

The forms of LORD and GOD in quotations from the Bible represent the Hebrew *Yahweh*, while Lord and God represent *Adonai*, in accordance with the Bible version used.

Excluding Scripture verses and deity pronouns, in some quotations references to men and masculine pronouns have been replaced with gender-neutral or feminine references. Additionally, in some cases we have carefully updated verb forms and wording that may distract modern readers.

Stock or custom editions of Summerside Press titles may be purchased in bulk for educational, business, ministry, fundraising, or sales promotional use. For information, please e-mail specialmarkets@summersidepress.com.

Cover design by Lookout Design, Inc.
Interior design and typesetting by Jeff Jansen | AestheticSoup.net

Summerside Press is an inspirational publisher offering fresh, irresistible books to uplift the heart and engage the mind.

Printed in China

Contents

Special Thanks

To my wife Leah, who is always the first to read or hear anything I create. You are my best friend and encourager. I couldn't do it without you!

To Micah, Maisie, and Wyatt—being your dad is the ultimate privilege. I love you!

To Krissy Nordhoff—what a privilege to have worked on this song together. I'm so thankful for you and Eric's friendship. I look forward to more writing in the future!

To Randy Elliott, Marilyn Jansen, Joanie Garborg, and Jason Rovenstine at Summerside Press—you were a joy to work with!

To Kurt Beasley, Chad Williams, and Brent Gray—I'm so thankful to work alongside you bringing stories and songs to the world. Your friendship is a gift.

To my pastor, mentor, and friend, Dr. J. Todd Mullins—I'm so grateful to do life and ministry with you. What a gift!

To my mentors, Dr. Tom "Coach" Mullins and Dr. John C. Maxwell—I'm blessed beyond words by your investment into my life!

What's in a Name?

In our twenty-first-century Western culture it seems little thought is given to the meaning of our names. I've heard young parents say, "We just liked the way that name sounded." This was not the case in biblical times. Naming carried special significance...it stood for something intentional and specific. God revealed His names to His people in Scripture. They did not name Him.

We call on His name.

We gather in His name.

We pray in His name.

We find hope in His name.

We love in His name.

We are saved through His name.

In this book, I hope you experience the ultimate power and unfathomable depth revealed in the names of God. His character and nature are unwavering.

In nearly every line of the song "Your Great Name," a name of God is echoed. We did not plan it that way in the writing process...but I believe the Holy Spirit did. His name—who He is—is unparalleled.

One day, as Philippians 2:10–11 says, "At the name of Jesus, every knee should bow...and every tongue acknowledge that Jesus Christ is Lord, to the glory of God the Father."

Lord, save us!

Lord, grant us success!

Blessed is he who comes in the name of the Lord.

Psalm 118:25–26

Chapter 1

Lost Are Saved

Your Great Name:

HOSANNA

Meaning:

LORD, SAVE US

LORD, SAVE US!

There is no one so far lost that Jesus cannot find him and cannot save him.

ANDREW MURRAY

"Hosanna! Blessed is He who comes in the name of the Lord!" The cry of the multitude echoed throughout Jerusalem as they welcomed Jesus with thunderous praise in Matthew 21:9. It says in the Scriptures that it "moved the city." Can you picture it? They were reverberating the Messianic Psalm of David, Psalm 118:25–26, which begs "LORD, save us! LORD, grant us success! Blessed is he who comes in the name of the LORD."

The Hebrew word for "Lord, save us" in this prophecy is *Hosanna*. Hosanna means "God, save us" or "Please save now." The children of Israel were recognizing they were in the presence of royalty that day. They were calling Him "Hosanna!" as a proclamation of praise, but the meaning held deep roots in their people's longing for salvation.

Breathless

To think about our God as Hosanna leaves me breathless at times. I feel like the psalmist in chapter 8:3–4: "When I consider your heavens, the work of your fingers, the moon and the stars, which you have set in place, what is mankind that you are mindful of them, human beings that you care for them?"

The maker of all things seen and unseen is deeply involved in our journey, more than we could ever imagine, and He *cares* for us. Psalm 34:18 says, "The Lord is close to the brokenhearted and *saves* (emphasis added) those who are crushed in spirit." Our Hosanna hears every cry, and not one tear falls without it moving His heart.

If you are brokenhearted today, cry out "Hosanna! Blessed is he who comes in the name of the Lord." He is the God who saves.

Rescued

[The Lord] reached down from on high and took hold of me;
he drew me out of deep waters....
The Lord was my support.
He...rescued me because he delighted in me.

Psalm 18:16, 18-19

Not too long ago I was at a birthday party for a close friend. It was a beautiful evening, and all of the parents were watching the young ones run around the backyard of the house by the glow of the tiki torches. The lingering smell of the barbecue grill was still in the air. At least a dozen or more kids were yelling and screaming, chasing each other around. It was pure mayhem, but joyful.

The festivities came to a screeching halt, however, when a loud shriek from a mother rang out, "Kevin! Meghan's in the pool!" I'll never forget what I saw: three-year-old Meghan, with her bright red pigtails, was struggling silently like a frantic marionette puppet, a few feet under water. Kevin, her father, who had only turned his back for a second, jumped in fully clothed, without hesitation, to save her.

Thankfully, Meghan was fine. She took on a little water but coughed it right out when they surfaced. Not a scene I'll ever forget.

When I think of Meghan, I think of us...humanity, you and me. We were underwater, no hope of survival, then our Father joined us... extended His arms to rescue us. Our Hosanna heard our cry, even before we were able to utter it. Through His shed blood on the cross and the power of the empty tomb, forever we are saved.

Hosanna! Lost are saved at the sound of His great name.

The most glorious promises of God are generally fulfilled in such a wondrous manner that He steps forth to save us at a time when there is the least appearance of it.

C. H. von Bogatzky

Hosanna

The LORD *is my shepherd,*

I shall not want.

He makes me lie down in green pastures;

He leads me beside quiet waters.

He restores my soul.

PSALM 23:1–3 NASB

Chapter 2

Find Their Way

Your Great Name:

Jehovah-Raah

Meaning:

The Lord My Shepherd

The Lord My Shepherd

One of the first passages of Scripture I learned as a child was Psalm 23. I'm so glad I did. It has come to the fore of my mind and heart many times in life.

Attributed to King David, this psalm is one of poetic beauty and profound comfort. Many scholars believe it may have been written during one of David's darkest hours, when Saul was in pursuit to murder him. It is evidence of David's great faith in God to shepherd him through what must have been an extremely difficult time in his life.

It is in those first five words that we can find another of God's names, *Jehovah-Raah*—the Lord is my shepherd. We are not alone in this world, left to wander aimlessly, unguided and unprotected. Our shepherd will take care of us...provide for us. This psalm is a declaration of trust in Jehovah-Raah.

Psalm 23

The Lord *is my shepherd; I shall not want.*

He maketh me to lie down in green pastures: he leadeth me beside the still waters.

He restoreth my soul: he leadeth me in the paths of righteousness for his name's sake.

Yea, though I walk through the valley of the shadow of death, I will fear no evil:

for thou art with me; thy rod and thy staff they comfort me.

Thou preparest a table before me in the presence of mine enemies:

thou anointest my head with oil; my cup runneth over.

Surely goodness and mercy shall follow me all the days of my life:

and I will dwell in the house of the Lord *for ever.*

Psalm 23 kjv

More Than Enough

I have received full payment and have more than enough.... And my God will meet all your needs according to the riches of his glory in Christ Jesus.

Philippians 4:18–19

Oh, what comfort to know God as Jehovah-Raah, the Lord our shepherd. Raah can further be translated as "friend"...the Lord my friend. Psalm 23 gives us a beautiful picture of friendship and intimacy in the midst of any circumstance. To me, one of the most moving things about this psalm of David is the declaration "You are with me." It's the promise of His presence in the dark times.

That promise also assures us that in our need, He is more than enough. He will be with us in all situations, providing what we need, showing us the way, carrying our grief.

In our need for provision: the Lord our shepherd leads us to green pastures and still waters, restoring our souls.

In our need for guidance: the Lord our shepherd leads us in the paths of righteousness for His name's sake.

In our need for comfort and peace: the Lord our shepherd is with us, in the valley or even in the face of death, sharing a meal of friendship, giving us all that we need and more.

Find rest today from Jesus' words in John 10:14–15: "I am the good shepherd; I know my sheep and my sheep know me—just as the Father knows me and I know the Father—and I lay down my life for the sheep."

We are not alone in the battle, in our grief, our suffering, or our pain. He is with us, and He is more than enough.

Abandon yourself to His care and guidance, as a sheep in the care of a shepherd, and trust Him utterly.

HANNAH WHITALL SMITH

Leaning On the Shepherd

As a shepherd looks after his scattered flock when he is with them, so will I look after my sheep. I will rescue them from all the places where they were scattered on a day of clouds and darkness.

Ezekiel 34:12

No words could describe the way it felt that day in the NICU of Miami Children's Hospital. A few of us were huddled together, praying...but mostly crying, as they took our friends' first baby boy off life support. The heart monitor stopped beeping. The breathing machine bellows slowed to a standstill. Nothing but the sound of our crying could be heard. Several surgeries to repair a heart defect were to no avail. I still remember the look in the heart surgeon's eyes as he removed the tubes from the little boy's body. He couldn't fix this one.

It's something that no parent, no person, should have to go through. In the midst of unimaginable pain, I watched our friends lean on Jehovah-Raah. They will never get over losing their child, but their shepherd continues to bring them grace, comfort, and strength to go on, to thrive, and to find new life in Him. He has led them to still waters. He is helping them find their way on the journey.

They have two more beautiful children now. Their lives are a trophy of God's glory as they speak of their journey, pointing people to Jesus.

Jehovah-Raah, the Lord is my shepherd. The lost will find their way at the sound of His great name.

When God has become our shepherd, our refuge, our fortress, then we can reach out to Him in the midst of a broken world and feel at home while still on the way.

HENRI J. M. NOUWEN

The LORD *said to him, "Peace! Do not be afraid. You are not going to die." So Gideon built an altar to the* LORD *there and called it The* LORD *Is Peace.*

JUDGES 6:23–24

Chapter 3

Every Fear Has No Place

Your Great Name:

Jehovah-Shalom

Meaning:

The Lord Is Peace

The Lord Is Our Peace

This is peace—to be able to sleep in the storm! In Christ, we are relaxed and at peace in the midst of the confusions, bewilderments, and perplexities of this life. The storm rages, but our hearts are at rest.

Billy Graham

Gideon was about to face one of the most ominous battles of his life. God had called him to deliver the children of Israel from the oppression of the Midianites. Gideon wrestled with God in Judges 6 as he tried to disqualify himself: "My clan is the weakest...and I am the least in my family."

I can only imagine the anxiety Gideon must have felt. If you are anything like me, you have many days when you don't even feel qualified to do the seemingly tame and safe things we do every day. I can't imagine the fear that began to overtake his heart and mind at the thought of what he'd been asked to do. But then the Lord spoke the words we all need to hear in Judges 6:16: "I will be with you."

The Lord went on to dispel Gideon's fear with a sign and an appearance from an angel. The Lord said, "Peace! Do not be afraid. You are not going to die." So Gideon built an altar there to the Lord and called it *Jehovah-Shalom*, the Lord is our peace.

[God] comforts. He lays His right hand on the soul wounded by weariness, or fear, or any kind of weakness at all. And He says, as if that one were the only soul in all the universe... "greatly beloved, fear not: peace be unto thee."

AMY CARMICHAEL

Peace in the Storm

Save us, Lord; we are perishing!

Matthew 8:25 NASB

The Lord is our peace in the midst of the storm. Many times He dispels the storm, the conflict, and the struggle. Other times He calms our hearts in the midst of difficulties. Many times we find ourselves sailing the ocean of life in the thick of a violent storm, being tossed about by the wind and waves of relationships gone awry, a series of poor decisions, a grim health report, a feeling of wandering, or a lack of direction.

In Matthew chapter 8, the account of Jesus and His disciples in the boat together seems to mirror what I feel during those tumultuous times in life. It seems to be a brief but poignant display of God's power when the disciples don't think He's paying attention. A furious storm descends upon them, the disciples are terrified, thinking they will surely be capsized and drowned, and Jesus...is asleep. Of course they wake Him in a panic, begging Jesus to rescue them. He reprimands them for their lack of faith and their worry. Then He rebukes the wind and waves, and they cease their churning.

I've always wondered what happened after the incidents in verses 26 and 27. I can picture Jesus saying, "Come on, guys! What are you worried about? Wind...waves...Enough!" Then He shakes His head, grins, and goes right back to sleep, while the disciples are looking at each other saying, "Did you see that?"

Sometimes we shake our fist at God and scream, "Wake up! Don't You know what's going on here?" He does. He's not surprised by anything. He's in the boat with us. Psalm 27:5 says, "For in the day of trouble he will keep me safe in his dwelling; he will hide me in the shelter of his sacred tent and set me high upon a rock."

The Shelter of His Wings

I long to dwell in your tent forever and take refuge in the shelter of your wings.
Psalm 61:4

The year 2005 set records for hurricanes in Florida. We experienced several direct hits in our area that year from such sweetly named storms as Wilma, Rita, and Irene. Many people lost everything, lived without power for weeks, and struggled to locate food, water, and fuel. Beyond the destruction of personal property, though, there are images, beautiful scenes, of those days that will forever be etched in my mind and heart. People came together and helped one another. The community rallied to meet the needs of the most desperate.

During one of the storms, my friends and I wanted to watch the ocean as it made landfall. The power of the storm even in its early stages was breathtaking. It transformed the tranquil seascape into a churning and violent force. The waves were crashing up over the pier and slamming into the wall.

In the midst of the mayhem, high above us in the large lighthouse, I noticed a large bird of prey sitting calmly, peacefully, in a small opening on the ledge opposite the ocean. Its feathers were tousled by the wind, yet it almost seemed to be watching the swirl below as if untouched by it. The lighthouse was a fortress, a strong tower that would withstand the brutality of nature's attack. I thought of the psalmist's cry in Psalm 61:2–4: "Lead me to the rock that is higher than I. For you have been my refuge, a strong tower against the foe. I...take refuge in the shelter of your wings."

Whatever storm you are facing today, call out to your Jehovah-Shalom, the Lord our peace. Find shelter and strength in His great name.

The L*ORD* *is my strength and my shield;*
my heart trusts in him, and he helps me.
My heart leaps for joy, and with my song I praise him....
Save your people and bless your inheritance;
be their shepherd and carry them forever.

PSALM 28:7, 9

Chapter 4

All the Weak Find Their Strength

Your Great Name:

Jehovah Ez-Lami

Meaning:

The Lord Is My Strength

The Lord Is My Strength

I don't think there is anyone who needs God's help and grace as much as I do. Sometimes I feel so helpless and weak. I think that is why God uses me. Because I cannot depend on my own strength, I rely on Him twenty-four hours a day.

Mother Teresa

The book of Psalms speaks to us intimately on many levels. It reflects our cry for God in the whole of human nature. These honest songs of the children of Israel are poetry rising up from the full gamut of our emotions. In Psalm 28:7 David declares, "The Lord is my strength (*Ez-Lami*) and my shield: my heart trusts in him, and he helps me. My heart leaps for joy, and with my song I praise him." Again in verse 8 he recognizes, "The Lord is the strength of his people." When we are weak and cannot find the strength to stand, we can trust in His strength, which is infinite and inexhaustible.

From the tiny birds of the air and from the fragile lilies of the field we learn the same truth, which is so important for those who desire a life of simple faith: God takes care of His own. He knows our needs. He anticipates our crises. He is moved by our weaknesses. He stands ready to come to our rescue. And at just the right moment He steps in and proves Himself as our faithful heavenly Father.

CHARLES R. SWINDOLL

Trust Me

Weakness is not a trait our society looks upon fondly. It is not something we like to admit. "Try harder," "think right," "work smarter." All good things, right? Of course, these aren't inherently bad things. In fact, we want to be hard workers, working wisely and thinking truthful thoughts about life and what God's Word says about it. What happens, though, when it's not enough? What happens when we do our best in every area of life but somehow find ourselves weak, worn out, and frustrated? What happens when life delivers blow after blow and we just don't know where to turn?

Paul shares with us some counterintuitive insight in 2 Corinthians 12. He speaks of some kind of disability of his body that torments him relentlessly. Many scholars believe it had to do with his eyesight. He begged the Lord to take away this weakness and make him strong to accomplish all he had been given to do for Christ. The Lord responded to him in verse 9: "My grace is sufficient for you, for my power is made perfect in weakness." Rather than making Paul stronger by removing his weakness, the Lord in effect said, "I'll be your strength. Trust Me."

In our trials, hardships, and difficulties, we can lean on Jehovah Ez-Lami, the Lord our strength. When we are weak, we can become a trophy of God's strength.

Knowing God is putting your trust in Him. Trust that He loves you and will provide for your every need.... Because of who He is we have every reason to feel respect for Him and show it in the way that we live. We no longer fear the unknown, fear the future, or fear our circumstances.

Tom Richards

One Day I'll Dance

I have a good friend named Cynthia. She's in her twenties now. I've known her for at least a dozen years. She never misses church, and she's always in the front row giving her all in worship and taking in every word of the sermon. She's an incredibly strong young woman and is incredibly intelligent. She loves to laugh and encourage people. Nearly every time I see her she is smiling and full of joy. She always asks about my family and how I'm doing, and she never misses a chance to pray for me. I always walk away lifted up from being in her presence.

Cynthia has cerebral palsy. She's confined to a wheelchair and is virtually helpless physically without the aid of her parents. Every word is a struggle to enunciate as she fights to control her muscle spasms. Somehow, though, through her physical prison, this angel brings light in the darkness.

It was my privilege to have Cynthia pray over me as I began a season of songwriting. It is an encounter I'll never forget. She begged God to pour out His Spirit upon all of us and asked Him to give me a measure of creativity I'd never had. I wept for a long time, for many reasons—my own self-centeredness and lack of faith and the beauty of the gift I was being given. I'll never forget the essence of part of her prayer. "Jesus, I don't know why You gave me this prison of a body, but I thank You. One day I'll dance and run before You, but for now, I know You are my strength." I saw true supernatural, God-given strength that day.

All the weak will find their strength at the sound of His great name.

Abraham called that place

The LORD Will Provide.

And to this day it is said,

"On the mountain of the LORD

it will be provided."

GENESIS 22:14

Chapter 5

Hungry Souls

Your Great Name:

Jehovah Jireh

Meaning:

The Lord Will Provide

Abraham's Obedience

A bone-chilling scene is recorded in Genesis 22. Abraham has been instructed by God to take his son Isaac—the promised one, the child he waited for, for twenty-five years—to the region of Moriah and sacrifice him as a burnt offering to the Lord. None of us this side of eternity can fathom obeying that command. The entire passage is a beautiful prophecy of what God had planned for us through the sacrifice of Jesus.

Abraham's obedience is staggering as they make the journey. "'The fire and wood are here,' Isaac said, 'but where is the lamb for the burnt offering?' Abraham answered, 'God himself will provide the lamb for the burnt offering, my son'" (Genesis 22:7–8). He builds the altar and binds his son to it. As he is preparing to slay his son in an act of uncompromising obedience, God calls to him from the heavens and turns Abraham's attention to a ram provided for the sacrifice. What an incredible picture of what would happen hundreds of years later, on that very hill. God would provide Himself, Jesus, as the sacrifice for us.

Abraham called the place *Jehovah Jireh*, which has come to be interpreted "the Lord will provide." Literally interpreted in the Hebrew it also means "the Lord sees." Jehovah Jireh sees our need—and provides—in every way.

If God wants you to do something, He'll make it possible for you to do it, but the grace He provides comes only with the task and cannot be stockpiled beforehand. We are dependent on Him from hour to hour, and the greater our awareness of this fact, the less likely we are to faint or fail in a crisis.

Louis Cassels

Don't Worry

Therefore I tell you, do not worry about your life, what you will eat or drink; or about your body, what you will wear. Is not life more than food, and the body more than clothes? Look at the birds of the air; they do not sow or reap or store away in barns, and yet your heavenly Father feeds them. Are you not much more valuable than they? Can any one of you by worrying add a single hour to your life?

Matthew 6:25–27

I didn't think I was a worrier, but I've been taking stock of what really preoccupies my mind and heart. Many times what I disguise as concern with "planning for the future" or for "the best interests of my family" really translates into worry—worry that we won't have enough, worry that I won't be enough, or worry that something will happen to my family. How do I know what I'm experiencing is worry? Well, I think because I let it steal my joy. Has this ever happened to you?

The first thing I do now when I start to experience worry or anxiety is to pray. "Don't worry about anything; instead, pray about every thing. Tell God what you need, and thank him for all he has done" (Philippians 4:6 NLT).

At the root of worry is a lack of trust that God will provide for us. Jesus tells us in Matthew 6 not to worry about what we will eat, drink, or wear, because He knows we need these things. He lovingly admonishes us to seek His kingdom and righteousness and those things will be given to us. He is reminding us that everything comes from Him. He is more than enough!

We are in need, hungry for provision in every area of our life. We need to look no further than Jesus.

Everything We Need

His divine power has given us everything we need for a godly life through our knowledge of him who called us by his own glory and goodness.

2 Peter 1:3

My kids get commissions for the work they do around the house. Once, at the end of the month (which equals payday to them), my two older ones came to me for the hefty payout. Grinning from ear to ear, they tucked their cash into their backpacks and headed to school. Later that day I arrived home and my kids proceeded to lay their earnings on the counter. "What's this, guys?" I asked. My oldest boy spoke up for himself and his little sister.

"We want you to have it. Thanks for working so hard for us."

I was moved deeply by their gratitude. "That money is yours. You earned it! Isn't there something you'd like to buy with it?"

Their reply was beautiful.

"You give us everything we need, Dad."

I'll never forget that exchange. It showed me that these little hearts had complete trust in me. They had faith that if they needed anything, it would be provided.

Oh, for us to have that kind of trust in our heavenly Father, who has more than we could ever dream of. He reminds us in Matthew 7:11 that if we—fallen, broken creatures—take care of our kids, how much more will He—who is perfect, holy, and full of unfailing love—care for us.

Hungry souls will have everything they need, at the sound of His great name.

The Spirit you received does not make you slaves, so that you live in fear again; rather, the Spirit you received brought about your adoption to sonship. And by him we cry, "Abba, Father."

Romans 8:15

CHAPTER 6

The Fatherless

Your Great Name:

ABBA

Meaning:

DADDY

Our Father

See what great love the Father has lavished on us,
that we should be called children of God! And that is what we are!

1 John 3:1

Abba, in the original language, is a more intimate, less formal word than Father. It's more like *Papa* or *Daddy*.

In Mark 14:36, we see this so powerfully in the Garden of Gethsemane when Jesus pours His heart out the night before His death. "Abba, Father [Daddy]," he said, "everything is possible for you. Take this cup from me. Yet not what I will, but what you will."

Because of what Jesus has done for us, and our trust in His perfect work, we have been brought into the family of God. All through Romans 8 Paul encourages us to accept that we are no longer enslaved to sin and that there is no condemnation in Christ Jesus. By the work of His Holy Spirit, we don't have to wander about powerless and full of fear. We are children of the King!

When Jesus taught us how to pray in Matthew 6:9, He led out with "Our Father...."

The prophet Isaiah declares in 9:6 that His name will be "Wonderful Counselor, Mighty God, Everlasting Father."

Many times we look at our heavenly Father through the lens of our experience with our earthly father. You may have had an abusive, aloof, or even absent father. Maybe you felt like you never measured up to your father's expectations. Whatever your experience with your earthly father is or isn't, it cannot compare to the riches of grace you have in your heavenly Father.

He will never leave us. He always has time. He is patient and kind, slow to anger, and rich in love. Oh, that we would, by the truth of His Word and the power of His Spirit, begin to know Him as our true Abba.

Father to the Fatherless

The fatherless, they find their rest, at the sound of Your great name.

Michael Neale and Krissy Nordhoff

A few years ago, a friend I've known since kindergarten met a very beautiful young lady and fell head over heels in love. He was in his early thirties, and it was wonderful to see how excited he was. What struck me about the relationship was that when they met, she was already pregnant...with another man's baby. It had been a one-night stand—a huge mistake. My friend didn't seem to mind. He loved her more than anything, and the pregnancy didn't deter him. I remember their baby boy being pulled in a wagon down the aisle with the flower girl the day they were wed. It really was a beautiful sight. My friend immediately filed to adopt that little boy and became his father.

But all too soon it came crashing down. Within months, the beautiful little family was torn apart when the mother said she didn't love my friend anymore and there was someone else. She left…and took her son with her. Most guys would have just moved on, but my friend has been a father to that boy since his birth. He continues to spend time with his adopted son eight years later, driving ten hours every weekend to spend time together. They go to football games, spend weekends and summers together, and they share an unbreakable bond.

It is a small picture of what God has done for us. In the midst of our broken world He came so we could be adopted into His family.

No one has to be fatherless at the sound of His great name.

"This is the land you are to allot as an inheritance to the tribes of Israel, and these will be their portions," declares the Sovereign Lord.... "And the name of the city from that time on will be: THE LORD IS THERE."

EZEKIEL 48:29, 35

Chapter 7

Rest in His Presence

Your Great Name:

Jehovah Shammah

Meaning:

The Lord Is There

The Lord Is with Me

Truly my soul finds rest in God;
my salvation comes from him.
Truly he is my rock and my salvation;
he is my fortress, I will never be shaken.

Psalm 62:1–2

In the last verse of the prophecy in Ezekiel 48 we see the final name of God recorded in the Old Testament: "The name of the city from that time on will be: THE LORD IS THERE" (*Jehovah Shammah*). What a powerful proclamation! The presence of God would reside with His people in Jerusalem during the time of the New Covenant as God's promises are fulfilled. He was with them and would be with them in the coming age. He would not abandon them. Because of His presence, they could rest in peace.

The psalmist reminds us of God's unfailing presence. "The LORD is with me; I will not be afraid. What can mere mortals do to me? The LORD is with me; he is my helper" (Psalm 118:6–7).

When we need to find peace and rest in a time of difficulty or suffering, it helps to journal our prayers to God. He knows what we need before we ask. He is there. His presence and promises are with us. If we reflect on those, our hearts can find rest.

The reflective life is a life that is attentive, receptive,
and responsive to what God is doing in us and around us.
It's a life that asks God to reach into our heart,
allowing Him to touch us there.

KEN GIRE

Secure in His Presence

The Lord replied, "My Presence will go with you, and I will give you rest."

Exodus 33:14

I have to travel occasionally to speak or lead worship, and while I love to see the world and meet new people, it is always a struggle to leave my family—for any length of time. I remember one time I was heading out to the airport and my children—we have three in elementary school—were lamenting my departure.

My little girl spoke up and said, "Daddy, I just don't sleep as good when you're not home." She went on to explain that when I was there, she felt more safe and secure and she knew she could call on me in the night if she needed to. It broke my heart. It did, however, help us take time as a family to talk about God and His presence with us no matter where we are.

We can rest, knowing that God's presence is with us, bringing comfort and protection from the Enemy. He is ever present. We can turn our fear over to Him and find rest at the sound of His great name.

God speaks to the crowd, but His call comes to individuals, and through their personal obedience He acts. He does not promise them nothing but success, or even final victory in this life.... God does not promise that He will protect them from trials, from material cares, from sickness, from physical or moral suffering. He promises only that He will be with them in all these trials, and that He will sustain them if they remain faithful to Him.

PAUL TOURNIER

The Lord...said, "If you listen carefully to the Lord *your God and do what is right in his eyes, if you pay attention to his commands and keep all his decrees, I will not bring on you any of the diseases I brought on the Egyptians, for I am the* Lord*, who heals you."*

Exodus 15:25–26

Chapter 8

The Sick Are Healed

Your Great Name:

Jehovah-Raphe

Meaning:

The Lord Who Heals

The Great Healer

In other religions, one must be purified before he can knock at the door; in Christianity, one knocks on the door as a sinner, and He who answers us heals.

Fulton J. Sheen

In this broken world, all are in need of healing...physical, emotional, and spiritual. God first reveals Himself as our healer in Exodus 15:26. God had just miraculously delivered the children of Israel from four hundred years of bondage in Egypt. Three days into their new freedom they were out of water, crying out, and complaining. Confirming that their desire was to walk faithfully in obedience to Him was of great importance to the Father. He told them that if they would heed His commands He would not plague them with the diseases that He had sent upon the Egyptians. He declared, "For I am the Lord who heals you."

Throughout the Bible are stories of healing, stories that reinforce the fact that God is the Great Healer. By His power we are healed. He takes away pain, sickness, death, and diseases of all kind. He is *Jehovah-Raphe*, the Lord who heals.

Praise the Lord, my soul;
all my inmost being, praise his holy name.
Praise the Lord, my soul,
and forget not all his benefits—
who forgives all your sins
and heals all your diseases,
who redeems your life from the pit
and crowns you with love and compassion,
who satisfies your desires with good things
so that your youth is renewed like the eagle's.

Psalm 103:1–5

Jesus Heals

But He was wounded for our transgressions,
He was bruised for our iniquities;
The chastisement for our peace was upon Him,
And by His stripes we are healed.

Isaiah 53:5 NKJV

As Jesus walked the earth, everywhere He went He brought healing. The lame, the blind, the demon-possessed, the diseased, and the broken-hearted found healing in Jehovah-Raphe.

He "went through all the towns and villages, teaching in their synagogues, proclaiming the good news of the kingdom and healing every disease and sickness. When he saw the crowds, he had compassion on them, because they were harassed and helpless, like sheep without a shepherd" (Matthew 9:35–36).

God has not changed. In our time, we don't see the answer we long for every time we pray for healing, but we know His name is still

Jehovah-Raphe. Even though we don't always understand, His timing and ways of healing seem to be infinite.

Sometimes we see the instantaneous healing from a disease or addiction, and sometimes it is slow and gradual through many avenues and circumstances. Oftentimes we may not see the healing this side of heaven, but we know He is making all things new! As Revelation 21:5 says, "He who was seated on the throne said, 'I am making everything new!' Then he said, 'Write this down, for these words are trustworthy and true.'"

Let the healing grace of Your love, O Lord, so transform me that I may play my part in the transfiguration of the world from a place of suffering, death, and corruption to a realm of infinite light, joy, and love. Make me so obedient to Your Spirit that my life may become a living prayer, and a witness to your unfailing presence.

MARTIN ISRAEL

God Healed It

Listen! The Lord's arm is not to weak to save you,
nor is his ear too deaf to hear you call.

Isaiah 59:1 NLT

We were all packed and ready to head out for vacation when we heard the scream from the back bedroom. Our oldest son, who was four at the time, decided to make a tower of chairs, toys, and boxes on top of his desk from which he could "fly" over to his bed. The tower crumbled underneath him and he fell on his elbow. It looked awful. It was swollen and he couldn't move it an inch.

We took him to the emergency room where they x-rayed it, confirmed it was broken, explained the severity of it, and told us to see an orthopedic surgeon on Monday. Our vacation would now be postponed for at least three days.

Then something amazing happened. The doctor came in after reviewing the files and asked, "How are you feeling, Micah?"

"I'm good. God healed it. I prayed," he said quite confidently.

"Really?" the Jewish doctor asked with a smile. He proceeded to take Micah's arm out of the temporary cast and asked him to move it. Micah wiggled his arm as if nothing was wrong and then asked, "Can we go on vacation now?"

His mother and I stared in disbelief. The doctor's eyebrows were raised. "Either his arm was never broken, or God did heal it."

We believe God heard the faith of our child that night. Whether it's physical, emotional, or spiritual healing, He is our Jehovah-Raphe. All will be healed and made new at the sound of His great name.

Thus says the Lord, your Redeemer,
And He who formed you from the womb:
"I am the Lord, who makes all things,
Who stretches out the heavens all alone,
Who spreads abroad the earth by Myself.

Isaiah 44:24 NKJV

CHAPTER 9

Redeemer

Your Great Name:

GA'AL

Meaning:

OUR REDEEMER

Our Redeemer

May these words of my mouth and this meditation of my heart be pleasing in your sight, Lord, my Rock and my Redeemer.

Psalm 19:14

One of the most beautiful names of God in Scripture to me is *Ga'al*, our Redeemer. In ancient biblical Hebrew culture, the kinsman-redeemer is the nearest relative of another, the one who is given the responsibility of restoring the rights of that person and avenging his or her wrongs.

In Leviticus 25:25 instructions are given for a kinsman to repurchase a field that was sold in time of need so the relative could go back to that land. Another helpful illustration is found in Leviticus 25:48: the call for a relative to redeem a kinsman who had to sell himself or herself into slavery to survive.

Throughout Scripture we see God referred to as the divine Ga'al, *our* Redeemer. What a powerful truth that causes us to respond in grateful praise!

When we focus on God, the scene changes. He's in control of our lives; nothing lies outside the realm of His redemptive grace. Even when we make mistakes, fail in relationships, or deliberately make bad choices, God can redeem us.

PENELOPE J. STOKES

Though you search for your enemies, you will not find them.
Those who wage war against you will be as nothing at all.
For I am the LORD your God who takes hold of
your right hand and says to you,
Do not fear; I will help you…
I myself will help you, declares the LORD,
your Redeemer, the Holy One of Israel.

ISAIAH 41:12–14

My People

Ruth said, "Do not urge me to leave you or turn back from following you; for where you go, I will go, and where you lodge, I will lodge. Your people shall be my people, and your God, my God. Where you die, I will die, and there I will be buried. Thus may the Lord do to me, and worse, if anything but death parts you and me."

Ruth 1:16–17 NASB

To know that our God is working on our behalf to restore us brings such hope. The same God who delivered Israel out of captivity is also delivering us and restoring us to our rightful place as sons and daughters of the Most High. He will avenge all the evil we have faced in this life.

The epic story in the book of Ruth shows the role of the kinsman-redeemer so beautifully. Ruth, a desperate widow, decides to stay with her widowed mother-in-law, Naomi, and return to Bethlehem with her. In Ruth 1:16 she declares her undying commitment. "Where you go, I will go, and where you stay, I will stay. Your people will be my people and your God my God."

This story of love and devotion leads to her marriage to a wealthy man named Boaz, by whom Ruth is rescued and redeemed. It's another beautiful picture of what Jesus has done for us!

God longs to give favor—that is, spiritual strength and health—to those who seek Him, and Him alone. He grants spiritual favors and victories, not because the one who seeks Him is holier than anyone else, but in order to make His holy beauty and His great redeeming power known.... For it is through the living witness of others that we are drawn to God at all. It is because of His creatures, and His work in them, that we come to praise Him.

St. Teresa of Avila

Redeemer

Repaired

They remembered that God was their Rock,
that God Most High was their Redeemer.

Psalm 78:35

I heard a story once of a young, single mother in a small church. She was in her late twenties, struggling just to get by. After a string of medical incidents, her only recourse to be able to pay the rent and put food on the table that month was to sell her car.

An older retired man in the church found out about what the young lady was going through and went to the dealership she sold her car to. He bought it back, put new tires on it, gave it a new paint job, had the engine tuned up, and returned it to her in nearly brand-new condition. Can you imagine? Not only did she have her car back but she also knew someone cared about her enough to do all of that!

A couple of years later that man could no longer drive himself around town, so in that very car, this same young lady gave him rides to the store and to doctor appointments. There was so much more to this story than repaired cars. It was more about repaired hearts.

Jesus came to buy back our broken hearts. We are redeemed at the sound of His great name.

Whatever your loss, pain, failure, or brokenness, Jesus Christ is fully capable of bringing about change unto full restoration. Just as His resurrection power brings new life, His redemption power brings new hope. He is able, for He's more than a Savior! He's your Redeemer who promises that He will give "beauty for ashes, the oil of joy for mourning" (Isaiah 61:3).

JACK HAYFORD

They remembered that God was their Rock, that God Most High [El Elyon] was their Redeemer.

Psalm 78:35

Chapter 10

Lord Almighty

Your Great Name:

El Elyon

Meaning:

God Most High

God Almighty

I cry out to God Most High, to God, who fulfills his purpose for me.

Psalm 57:2

Our God is the Almighty, the Most High. There is nothing and no one above Him. He is the great I Am and the Lord of all things seen and unseen. The first appearance of His name *El Elyon*, the God Most High, is in Genesis 14:18–20, a fascinating passage of Scripture! A mysterious king named Melchizedek, whom we know very little about, appears in the Scriptures. It's interesting to me that after Melchizedek blessed Abraham, Abraham gave him a tenth of all he owned, showing that he viewed him as a very important or high-ranking person. He is said to be a priest of El Elyon, the Most High, and many scholars believe this could have been a pre-incarnate appearance of Jesus Himself!

More than two dozen times God is revealed in Scripture as El Elyon. When the storm gets rough, the waves get high, the wind is strong, and the trial seems too much to bear, we can rest in the truth that our God has all authority and power over every circumstance. Nothing surprises Him. He is outside of time and space. He knows the end from the beginning. He is the Most High, and He is on our side!

Then Melchizedek king of Salem brought out bread and wine.
He was priest of God Most High,
and he blessed Abram, saying,
"Blessed be Abram by God Most High,
Creator of heaven and earth.
And praise be to God Most High,
who delivered your enemies into your hand."

Genesis 14:18–20

All Things

"It is easier for a camel to go through the eye of a needle than for someone who is rich to enter the kingdom of God." When the disciples heard this, they were greatly astonished and asked, "Who then can be saved?" Jesus looked at them and said, "With man this is impossible, but with God all things are possible."

Matthew 19:24–26

In Matthew, there is a story about a rich man who asks how to achieve eternal live. Jesus tells him to sell his possessions, which he refuses to do. The disciples question Jesus about who could be saved if it is so difficult to achieve. He looks at them and says, "With man this is impossible, but with God all things are possible" (Matthew 19:26).

Think about that for a minute. With God, *ALL* things are possible! There is nothing out of the scope of His power to accomplish or create. If there is something in our lives that seems impossible—

a relationship, a financial struggle, an illness—whatever it may be, we can give it to the Lord. We can declare *His* strength in the middle of the situation. He may not choose to remove the struggle, but He will give us the strength to overcome. He is our God Most High!

Let's praise His name! He is holy, He is almighty. He is love. He brings hope, forgiveness, heart cleansing, peace, and power. He is our deliverer and coming King. Praise His wonderful name!

LUCILLE M. LAW

El Elyon

Safe in the Almighty

The Lord your God is in your midst, the mighty one will save;
He will rejoice over you with gladness; He will quiet you with his love;
He will rejoice over you with singing.

Zephaniah 3:17 NKJV

A few years ago, my band, Neale and Webb, was in Belgrade, Serbia, at the invitation of the prime minister of education. We were to play music for the students in the public schools and do a concert in the soccer stadium on the weekend.

One unfortunate day our over-zealous interpreter had a run-in with the headmaster, accusing him of not letting us in because we were Christian. The police were called, we didn't have our passports (we were told to lock them in the hotel), and the drummer and I ended up in a Serbian jail.

For several hours we were interrogated in a smoky room with one bare lightbulb hanging down and a dozen officers. We sat next to criminals in chains who were getting beaten bloody during their interrogations. You'd better believe we were crying out for our God Most High. Just when it was again our turn for interrogation, an ambassador from the US embassy showed up and negotiated our release. We were so relieved.

Later that night, every one of those officers showed up for security detail at our concert. They heard the gospel that night as we lifted up the great name of Jesus. You just never know what God is up to!

We will see Him as Lord Almighty—El Elyon—at the sound of His great name!

She will give birth to a son, and you are to give him the name Jesus [Yeshua], because He will save His people from their sins.

Matthew 1:21

CHAPTER 11

My Savior

Your Great Name:

YESHUA

Meaning:

JESUS, SAVIOR

Call Him Jesus

Therefore, there is now no condemnation for those who are in Christ Jesus, because through Christ Jesus the law of the Spirit who gives life has set you free from the law of sin and death.

Romans 8:1–2

Yeshua means Salvation. Yeshua is the Hebrew name for our Savior, Jesus. It is the name the angel told Mary to give to her son. It is the name that saves.

Jesus alone is our rescuer. We were separated from God because of sin. God is holy and perfect, so justice had to be done for infinite love to be displayed. All of this came through the sacrifice of our Yeshua. The cross rings through all eternity as a declaration of the saving grace of God.

This is a gift from God that is available to anyone who wishes to receive it. When we admit personally that we are sinners and surrender our lives to Him, He will rescue us! Romans 8:1 says there is then "no condemnation for those who are in Christ Jesus."

Yeshua comforted His disciples as He told them of a place He was going to prepare for them. Thomas wanted to know the way there. And Yeshua replied, "I am the way and the truth and the life. No one comes to the Father except through me" (John 14:6).

If you have never put your trust in Yeshua and His saving power you can...right now. You can call out to Him, ask forgiveness of your sin, declare your need of Him, and trust His saving work on the cross for you. He will answer.

Never were God's arms opened so wide as they were on the Roman cross.
One arm extending back into history and the other reaching into the future.
An embrace of forgiveness offered for anyone who'll come.
A hen gathering her chicks. A father receiving his own.
A redeemer redeeming the world. No wonder they call Him the Savior.

MAX LUCADO

God-Given Purpose

We neither make nor save ourselves. God does both the making and saving. He creates each of us by Christ Jesus to join him in the work he does, the good work he has gotten ready for us to do, work we had better be doing.... God is building a home. He's using us all—irrespective of how we got here—in what he is building. He used the apostles and prophets for the foundation. Now he's using you, fitting you in brick by brick, stone by stone, with Christ Jesus as the cornerstone that holds all the parts together.

Ephesians 2:10, 19–21 msg

I was nine years old, sitting in the back row of our little country church, when I knew what I was going to do with my life.

There was a family that would frequently stop at our little church for revival meetings. This family was so inspiring. The children would sing, the mom played the piano, and the dad would preach. I remember thinking, *I would love to get on a bus, to travel around and play music for people someday; that is the life!* I had no idea that was a God-given desire.

I don't remember everything about the last night of the revival, but I do remember the preacher telling the story of how Jesus saves us.

I remember the presence of God overwhelming me and getting a glimpse of His love and power. The tears flowed. I *knew* He was my Savior. I went to the altar and gave Him my heart. I confessed my past and my need for Him, and I dedicated my future days to Him. I felt like a new person. I *was* a new person.

Following Him for thirty years has been breathtaking. Life is hard, but I have a purpose. I'm a child of Yeshua, my Savior. I live to know Him...and make Him known.

We are saved by His great name!

Don't be afraid, I've redeemed you. I've called your name. You're mine.... I am God, your personal God, the Holy of Israel, your Savior. I paid a huge price for you...! That's how much you mean to me! That's how much I love you!

ISAIAH 43:1–4 MSG

In those days Judah will be saved
and Jerusalem will live in safety.
This is the name by which it will be called:
The LORD Our Righteous Savior.

JEREMIAH 33:16

Chapter 12

The Condemned Feel No Shame

Your Great Name:

Jehovah Tsidkenu

Meaning:

Lord of Righteousness

No Shame

The Lord *Almighty will be exalted by his justice, and the holy God will be proved holy by his righteous acts.*

Isaiah 5:16

Shame is brutal. We all wear it at some point or another. It is that awareness and feeling of unworthiness, disgrace, dishonor, embarrassment, and self-loathing. It is a very real thing to feel shame in the midst of humanity's predicament. Our souls long to be in harmony and relationship with our Creator. That's how we were "wired."

In and of ourselves, we are not in right standing with a holy and perfect God. We were born into a sin-filled world. Sin is the very thing that separated us from our destiny—to be in communion with God.

The good news is that someone came to take on our sin...and destroy it! The prophet Jeremiah, in chapter 23:5–6 (and in 33:16), foretold of the coming of *Jehovah Tsidkenu*, the Lord our Righteousness: "The days are coming," declares the Lord, "when I will raise up for David a righteous Branch, a King who will reign wisely and do what is just and right in the land.... This is the name by which he will be called: The LORD Our Righteous Savior." Jesus would come and be our righteousness for us. Because of Him, we could be made right again. The "guilty" verdict rendered in the Garden of Eden has been revoked eternally, all because of Jesus.

"Jehovah our righteousness." This is the grappling iron with which we get a hold on Him—this is the anchor which dives into the bottom of this great deep of His immaculate righteousness. This is the saved rivet by which our souls are joined to Him. This is the blessed hand with which our soul touches Him, and He becomes to us all in all, "Jehovah our Righteousness."

CHARLES H. SPURGEON

Jehovah Tsidkenu

Completely Free

Let us run with patience the race that is set before us, looking unto Jesus the author and finisher of our faith; who for the joy that was set before him endured the cross, despising the shame, and is set down at the right hand of the throne of God.

Hebrews 12:1–2 KJV

There's nothing better than a clear conscience. To have those seasons of freedom where we are not haunted by our past, we are living in the light and not afraid of what someone might find out about us—it's like walking on air. It's effortless and full of joy.

For many of us, we don't live in this space. Why? Many reasons, I'm sure. But regardless of what is keeping us mired in shame, we can overcome it with the help of the Lord of Righteousness. He takes our guilt so we can live completely free...completely forgiven...completely loved as we trust in Jesus and what He has done.

To understand the power of Jehovah Tsidkenu is to understand the problem. The truth is, we are hopeless to save ourselves from the quicksand of self and sin. This is the amazing news of Jesus. He is the remedy. In Colossians 1:21–22, Paul reminds us, "Once you were alienated from God and were enemies in your minds because of your evil behavior. But now he has reconciled you by Christ's physical body through death to present you holy in his sight, without blemish and free from accusation." We stand in the presence of God without accusation. Again, we are completely free...completely forgiven... completely loved when we trust in Jesus and what He has done.

There is no guilt inside the love of Jesus. He gives us our worth because of His unfailing love towards us. He gives us our destiny and purpose. He gives us our right standing with God. We can live a bold and joyful life because of everything Jesus has done for us. By God's grace, we can learn to trust in our Jehovah Tsidkenu, the Lord our Righteousness.

Melting Away

This righteousness is given through faith in Jesus Christ to all who believe.

Romans 3:22

I grew up in a small country church where Sundays were more like large family gatherings than church. One rainy Sunday when I was about nine years old, at the end of the second hymn I noticed that something had caught the eye of the song leader, Mr. Jamison. He glanced at the back door more than once. Many of us turned to discover a man who had bloodshot eyes, hair down to the middle of his back, a disheveled beard, and tattoos covering both arms.

The man got hugs from lots of folks and sat down with us to eat in the fellowship hall after the service. Mr. Jamison stood up. "May I have your attention everybody? Today, the Lord answered our prayers. My little brother Jerry has had a rough go of it. He's been away for a while. But today, he came home." His eyes filled with tears as he continued. "As we thank God for the food today, I'm thanking God that my little brother is home!" Everybody clapped their hands and gave a good "Amen!"

I found out later that Jerry had struggled with drugs and alcohol, and his life was a mess. That day, he met Jesus...and even a nine-year-old boy could feel that his shame was melting away. All condemned feel no shame at the sound of His great name.

We are forgiven and righteous because of Christ's sacrifice; therefore we are pleasing to God in spite of our failures. Christ alone is the source of our forgiveness, freedom, joy, and purpose.

ROBERT S. McGEE

Jehovah Tsidkenu

You come against me with sword and spear and javelin, but I come against you in the name of the LORD Almighty, the God of the armies of Israel.

1 SAMUEL 17:45

CHAPTER 13

The Enemy Has to Flee

Your Great Name:

JEHOVAH SABAOTH

Meaning:

LORD OF HOSTS

Our Commander

You must not fear them, for the LORD *your God Himself fights for you.*

Deuteronomy 3:22 NKJV

Jehovah Sabaoth, the Lord of Hosts, appears more than 280 times in Scripture. Sabaoth means "armies" or "hosts." This name of God reveals Him as the universal sovereign commander of every army, both spiritual and mortal. He is the King over all heaven and earth.

The prophet Isaiah had a revelation about the throne of God in chapter 6 when he saw God as the Lord of Hosts—commander of the armies. The description of the seraphim as they worshiped, the scene of God's majestic throne and robe, and the crushing weight of His holiness is felt by Isaiah as he cries out in verse 5, "Woe is me, for I am undone! Because I am a man of unclean lips, and I dwell in the midst of a people of unclean lips; for my eyes have seen the King, the LORD of Hosts" (NKJV). Isaiah recognized God as Jehovah Sabaoth, commander of all, and the leader no enemy will stand against!

Final victory is ours, if we only remember that we are fighting God's battles. And can He know defeat? He who is the God of the great world around us is the God of the little world within. It is He who is contending in you; you are but His soldier, guided by His wisdom, strengthened by His might, shielded by His love. Keep your will united to the will of God, and the final defeat is impossible; for He is invincible.

George Body

At War

For our struggle is not against flesh and blood, but against the rulers, against the authorities, against the powers of this dark world and against the spiritual forces of evil in the heavenly realms. Therefore put on the full armor of God, so that when the day of evil comes, you may be able to stand your ground, and after you have done everything, to stand.

Ephesians 6:12–13

We are at war. The Enemy of our souls is attacking our families, our marriages, our faith, our integrity, our purpose, and our hope. He is trying to "devour" our very being. We must be vigilant and keep watch, looking beyond the temptation to self-destruct and give in to the real Enemy trying to deceive us.

In Ephesians 6:11, Paul reminds us to "put on the full armor of God, so that you can take your stand against the devil's schemes." With His armor we can defeat any temptation Satan throws at us. We will overcome deception when we rely on Jehovah Sabaoth. The Lord of Hosts is on our side and is for us! We can stand behind the shield of our King and Commander. Lord Sabaoth is His great name.

You, dear children, are from God and have overcome them, because the one who is in you is greater than the one who is in the world.

1 JOHN 4:4

When we are told that God, who is our dwelling place, is also our fortress, it can only mean one thing, and that is, that if we will but live in our dwelling place, we shall be perfectly safe and secure from every assault of every possible enemy that can attack us.

HANNAH WHITALL SMITH

On the Run

Lord, be merciful to us,
for we have waited for you.
Be our strong arm each day
and our salvation in times of trouble.
The enemy runs at the sound of your voice.
When you stand up, the nations flee!

Isaiah 33:2–3 NLT

Over a decade ago, evil manifested itself in a cowardly attack on innocent lives in New York City. No one can forget the horrific images of 9/11. Commercial airliners flying into the World Trade Center buildings, New York covered in soot and ash, families watching as loved ones perished—it all seemed otherworldly as these icons of American strength and commerce came crashing down.

America's resolve to bring the perpetrators to justice was and is unrelenting. Every military organization and intelligence agency was marshaled to find these evildoers. I remember watching news programs and documentaries of the enemy running and hiding in remote deserts and mountains, in areas highly populated by children and women, anywhere they could go to avoid the wrath of a superpower. They will be on the run forever...they will never enjoy rest. They have to flee.

From the cross (where Jesus sacrificed Himself to display infinite love and satisfy justice on our behalf) to the empty tomb (where He defeated death, hell, and the grave) Jehovah Sabaoth brought the full weight of His power to destroy the Enemy. His sacrifice put His enemies on the run. Our God is infinitely greater, and the Enemy flees when he hears His great name.

The Enemy; he has to leave;
at the sound of Your great name.

MICHAEL NEALE AND KRISSY NORDHOFF

Jehovah Sabaoth

You, Lord, are a compassionate and gracious God,
slow to anger, abounding in love and faithfulness.
Turn to me and have mercy on me;
show your strength in behalf of your servant;
save me, because I serve you.

Psalm 86:15–16

CHAPTER 14

Receive Grace

Your Great Name:

EL CHANNUN

Meaning:

GOD OF GRACE

God of Grace

The Lord, the Lord, [is] the compassionate and gracious God, slow to anger, abounding in love and faithfulness, maintaining love to thousands, and forgiving wickedness, rebellion and sin.

Exodus 34:6–7

In a fit of anger, while yelling at God, Jonah can't believe God would withhold His wrath on Nineveh. They were a brutal, violent, and idol-worshiping people who eventually listened to the reluctant missionary and turned from their evil ways. In his tirade in Jonah 4:2, as if to say "I knew this would happen!" he declares God as *El Channun*—God of grace: "I knew that you are a gracious and compassionate God, slow to anger and abounding in love, a God who relents from sending calamity." (See also Exodus 34:6, Numbers 14:18, and Psalm 86:15.)

I am so thankful for what we see all through Scripture, that God deals with us based on who He is—God of grace—not based on what we have done.

Grace is a marvelous but elusive word. "Unmerited favor" is the definition most of us know. It means self-giving, too, and springs from the person's own being without condition or consideration of whether the object is deserving. Grace may be unnoticed. But there are usually some who will notice. And those who are in a desperation of suffering will notice it, will notice even its lightest touch, and will hold it a precious and incalculably valuable thing.

Elisabeth Elliot

Grow in Grace

Grow in the grace and knowledge of our Lord and Savior Jesus Christ. To him be glory both now and forever!

2 Peter 3:18

In three words, grace is "God's unmerited favor." I've also heard the acronym "God's Riches At Christ's Expense." A. W. Tozer writes, "It is the good pleasure of God that inclines Him to bestow benefits on the undeserving." Throughout biblical history, we see the thread of God's grace toward us. Like the melodic theme of a symphonic masterpiece, it recurs in variations, singing over us, weaving together the story of God's love for His people.

"For it is by grace you have been saved, through faith, and this is not from yourselves, it is the gift of God" (Ephesians 2:8). The ultimate act of grace is our salvation! God's grace is alive and at work in us. It is not a one-time event but the ever-flowing power at work in us by the Holy Spirit. We stand in grace (Romans 5:2). We are strengthened by grace (Hebrews 13:9). We are encouraged to grow in grace: "But grow in the grace and knowledge of our Lord and Savior Jesus Christ" (2 Peter 3:18).

The entire life of following Jesus is only possible by the grace of God. It all starts and ends with Him.

From God, great and small, rich and poor, draw living water from a living spring, and those who serve Him freely and gladly will receive grace answering to grace.

THOMAS À KEMPIS

God of Grace

Extending Grace

Truly I tell you, whatever you did for one of the least of these brothers and sisters of mine, you did for me.

Matthew 25:40

When I was a young boy, my father was always looking for ways to help someone. We didn't have much compared to most of the folks we knew, certainly no excess, but that never stopped my dad.

One hot summer day we passed a homeless man trudging down the side of the highway. The middle-aged African-American man wore tattered pants, a dirty flannel shirt, and boots worn thin from walking the streets. I remember my dad looking in his rearview mirror as we passed the man and pulling over.

"Need a ride?"

The man looked surprised. "Sure!" He introduced himself as Earl and gave us directions to his destination. Dad conveniently stopped by our house first. I remember him offering Earl food and clean clothes, and talking with Earl about how much Jesus loved him. When we took Earl to his destination later that evening, he looked at Dad and said, "I thank you for your kindness, Bob." My dad was just doing what was in his nature to do—showing kindness and compassion to a man who couldn't offer anything in return but gratitude.

God, in infinite ways, has revealed and is continuing to reveal Himself as El Channun—the God of grace. He shows us love and favor even when we don't deserve it. Grace is ours at the sound of His great name.

God created mankind in his own image,
in the image of God he created them;
male and female he created them.

Genesis 1:27

Chapter 15

The Dead Are Raised

Your Great Name:

Elohim

Meaning:

All-Powerful God

Elohim

POWERFUL ONE

[Joshua] said to the Israelites, "In the future when your descendants ask their parents, 'What do these stones mean?' tell them, 'Israel crossed the Jordan on dry ground.' The LORD your God dried up the Jordan before you until you had crossed over.... He did this so that all the peoples of the earth might know that the hand of the LORD is powerful and so that you might always fear the LORD your God."

JOSHUA 4:21–24

Over 2,600 times in Scripture God refers to Himself or is referred to as *Elohim*, which means "God." It implies divine creativity and is the very first reference to God in the Bible: "In the beginning God created the heavens and the earth" (Genesis 1:1). Elohim is the all-powerful, divine creator and judge of the universe. In this name, God reveals Himself as the only God there is, the one with power to bring life from nothingness! He is the indisputable authority over all things seen and unseen.

His power is beyond our imagination. He can give life to a dead person and make a dry pathway across a raging sea. Yet because of His love, He offers abundant life. Our all-powerful God uses His power to give us eternal life!

Jesus the One and Only—the title is His forever. He was the One and Only long before He breathed a soul into humanity, and He will continue to be the One and Only long after the last soul has been judged. He is changeless. But you and I were destined for change. So determined is God to transform us, we cannot draw near Him and remain the same.

Beth Moore

Jesus Lives in Us

If the Spirit of him who raised Jesus from the dead is living in you, he who raised Christ from the dead will also give life to your mortal bodies because of his Spirit who lives in you.

Romans 8:11

An amazing story is recorded in John 11. Jesus' close friend Lazarus had died. When Jesus arrived, Lazarus had been in the grave four days. Martha came to meet him and said, "If only You'd been here, Lord, my brother would never have died. And I know that, even now, God will give You whatever You ask from Him." Jesus replied to her, "Your brother will rise again." Martha thought Jesus was talking about resurrection and the last days, but He said to her, "I myself am the resurrection and the life."

The story goes on as Jesus weeps over the death of His friend and then calls for the stone to be taken away. Can you imagine what it must have been like? Jesus calls for Lazarus to come out of the tomb and he does! This was a physical manifestation of Elohim's power over death.

Jesus Himself conquered death, hell, and the grave. Nothing could hold Him down. He rose from the grave on that third victorious day. And now that same power that raised Jesus from the dead lives in us! We don't have to be chained to sin and death any longer.

Jesus is the Savior, but He is even more than that! He is more than a Forgiver of our sins. He is even more than our Provider of eternal life. He is our Redeemer! He is the One who is ready to recover and restore what the power of sin and death has taken from us.

Jack Hayford

Life-Giving Love

I myself am he! There is no god besides me. I put to death and I bring to life, I have wounded and I will heal, and no one can deliver out of my hand.

Deuteronomy 32:39

“I was a walking dead man.” That was the phrase that stuck with me from my friend’s testimony that night at Believers in Recovery. After I led worship, I sat and listened to him unpack his journey. By all outward appearances you’d never know the hell he’d been through.

He was a child of an alcoholic and abusive father. As he came of age, he became addicted to drugs and alcohol and he described his life as meaningless and empty. He was depressed, he felt forgotten and abandoned, and he was walking through life void of any purpose and feeling. He had numbed the pain through every avenue of pleasure he could find, and he was still a walking dead man.

Then he was introduced to the life-giving love and power of Jesus through the woman who would become his wife. He said, "I came alive to what Jesus had done for me. I knew I was loved, I had a purpose, and I didn't need to be a slave to my past any longer. I was alive!"

The dead are raised at the sound of His great name!

A living, loving God can and does make His presence felt, can and does speak to us in the silence of our hearts, can and does warm and caress us till we no longer doubt that He is near, that He is here.

Brennan Manning

Elohim

Behold, a virgin shall be with child, and shall bring forth a son, and they shall call his name Emmanuel, which being interpreted is, God with us.

Matthew 1:23 KJV

Chapter 16

Never Alone

Your Great Name:

EMMANUEL

Meaning:

GOD WITH US

Close to Us

The righteous cry out, and the Lord *hears them; he delivers them from all their troubles. The* Lord *is close to the brokenhearted and saves those who are crushed in spirit. The righteous person may have many troubles, but the* Lord *delivers him from them all.*

Psalm 34:17–19

In the prophecy of Isaiah 7:14, the good news is declared that "[They] shall call His name Immanuel" (NKJV), which is translated, God with us. This is humanity's greatest news—that almighty God would not leave us alone, but He would be with us, among us, watching us, guiding us, healing us, and saving us.

God reveals His loving and compassionate presence for those who are under the weight of brokenness. It is impossible to escape having your heart broken this side of heaven. We may be brokenhearted from the betrayal of a friend or spouse, the death of a loved one, the loss of a job, or the shame of past failures. Jesus is close to us. He is acquainted with our suffering. *Emmanuel* is with us and will bring beauty out of the ashes as we trust Him.

I am with you, watching over you constantly. I am Emmanuel (God with you); My Presence enfolds you in radiant Love. Nothing, including the brightest blessings and the darkest trials, can separate you from Me.... I know precisely what you need to draw nearer to Me. Go through each day looking for what I have prepared for you.... Find Me in every situation.

SARAH YOUNG

His Healing Presence

He was despised and rejected by mankind, a man of suffering, and familiar with pain.... By his wounds, we are healed.

Isaiah 53:3, 5

In the quietness of this moment, consider that Jesus knows our deepest needs. He knows what it is like to be in our shoes. He understands the temptations and frustrations that we deal with. He is walking with us, closer than we can imagine, even in the darkest times. We can find healing as we lean on Emmanuel.

Even in the very worst situations, we are told not to be afraid, simply because He is with us. "Even though I walk through the darkest valley, I will fear no evil, for you are with me; your rod and your staff, they comfort me" (Psalm 23:4).

His presence is more than enough...just to be close to Him. He alone can heal our hearts. But whether He is here to heal or here to comfort us as we go through our brokenness, our God is with us. We never have to go through it alone. He knows and He is with us.

If God is present at every point in space, if we cannot go where He is not, cannot even conceive of a place where He is not, when then has not that Presence become the one unanswerably celebrated fact of the world?... People do not know if God is here. What a difference it would make if they knew.

A. W. Tozer

Sleep in Peace

Answer me when I call to you my righteous God.
Give me relief from my distress;
Have mercy on me and hear my prayer....
In peace I will lie down and sleep,
for you alone, LORD,
make me dwell in safety.

PSALM 4:1,8

Having three children is one of the greatest joys of my life. To see and experience life through their eyes, to watch them grow and learn, and to meet their needs is simply the best.

Our youngest, who is three, occasionally wakes up in the middle of the night screaming due to a bad dream. You can't really reason with him during that time. He's not fully coherent. But as soon as I pick him up and hold him close, he begins to calm. Even though he's not awake, he senses I'm there. He puts his head on my chest and can feel my heartbeat. He immediately quiets down and finds peace in my arms.

Our heavenly Father loves to be close to us...holding us in the midst of those times when we are scared, hurt, or confused. Our God is with us. Our minds and hearts are healed at the sound of His great name.

Incredible as it may seem, God wants our companionship. He wants to have us close to Him. He wants to be a father to us, to shield us, to protect us, to counsel us, and to guide us in our way through life.

Billy Graham

Moses built an altar and called it The Lord is my Banner. He said, "Because hands were lifted up against the throne of the Lord, the Lord will be at war against the Amalekites from generation to generation."

Exodus 17:15–16

Chapter 17

Defender

Your Great Name:

Jehovah Nissi

Meaning:

The Lord Our Banner

The Battle Won

May we shout for joy over your victory
and lift up our banners in the name of our God.

Psalm 20:5

Israel, wandering in the wilderness after miraculously crossing the Red Sea and escaping the Egyptian army, faced another formidable foe, the Amalekites. The story is recorded in Exodus 17, where Moses called on Joshua to lead the Israelites into battle against them while he went to the hilltop to lift his hands to pray.

As long as Moses held up his hands, the Israelites had the winning edge. Whenever Moses grew weary and his hands fell, the Amalekites would surge ahead. So Aaron and Hur held his hands up for him, and the battle was finally won! Moses constructed an altar there and called it *Jehovah Nissi*, the Lord Our Banner.

In biblical times, altars were often used to mark a significant event or a place of remembrance. These are places where God revealed Himself as defender and victor over every battle.

Flags or banners communicate in a number of ways. They unite us under our country's colors, they defy the enemy, and they ultimately signal victory on the battlefield. The Lord our banner flies over us in victory, protection, and power!

As we trust the Lord to provide, we gain the "inheritance" He makes possible as He fights the battles and wins the territory.... We don't have to be preoccupied with protecting our rights or grappling for control; the Lord enables us to inherit whatever "land" we need.

CHARLES R. SWINDOLL

We Are Victors

In my distress I called to the Lord; I cried to my God for help. From his temple he heard my voice; my cry came before him, into his ears.

Psalm 18:6

In Exodus 17:16, the Lord declares He will "be at war against the Amalekites from generation to generation." Many scholars believe the Amalekites represent the battle against the Enemy of our souls and the flesh. Jehovah Nissi will be our victory in every battle that we face today.

What does today's battle look like? We may be battling pride, envy, hopelessness, injustice, or depression. We could be battling with an illness, addiction, or financial difficulties. We are all in a battle. But we can lift our hands like Moses did and cry out for Jehovah Nissi. We can invite trusted friends like Aaron and Hur to lift our arms up in prayer. The Lord our banner will meet us.

We can rejoice and be glad that God has put His banner over us. We are victors because of His leadership. With Him, the battle is already won.

> *Grasp the fact that God is for you—let this certainty make its impact on you in relation to what you are up against at this very moment; and you will find in thus knowing God as your sovereign protector, irrevocably committed to you in the covenant of grace, both freedom from fear and new strength for the fight.*
>
> J. I. Packer

Victory

With God we will gain the victory, and he will trample down our enemies.

Psalm 60:12

I loved to sit and listen to my grandfather tell me stories. I remember sitting by his wood-burning stove and hearing about the Great Depression, funny mishaps from his travels, or historical events from early years. He had bookcases full of old US history and war books that fascinated me as a young boy.

I'll never forget the first time I opened one of his Time Life books on World War II and saw the Pulitzer Prize–winning photo called *Raising the Flag on Iwo Jima*. It has become a national symbol of courage, bravery, and victory for the United States. Grandpa's eyes would well up when he saw that photo.

Many times I've pictured myself as one of those soldiers on the battlefield of life, driving the flag of truth into the ground as a memorial for victory—victory because of my God, who in grace and power

You can fight with confidence where you are sure of victory. With Christ and for Christ victory is certain.

St. Bernard of Clairvaux

faithfully defends me from every attack. With every thankful prayer, every extended hand in worship, every meditation on His Word, we fly the flag over our lives and shout His great name, Jehovah Nissi, the Lord Our Banner!

We follow in procession behind a triumphant Christ! And if all our reliance is placed upon Him, we need never be defeated in spirit. Today, from hour to hour, He can and will lead us on to triumph—if we look to Him.

Amy Carmichael

Jehovah Nissi

To the Lord your God belong the heavens, even the highest heavens, the earth and everything in it.... For the Lord your God is God of gods and Lord of lords, the great God, mighty and awesome, who shows no partiality and accepts no bribes.

Deuteronomy 10:14, 17

Chapter 18

You Are My King

Your Great Name:

Adonai

Meaning:

Lord Master

MASTER OF ALL

Yours, LORD, is the greatness and the power and the glory and the majesty and the splendor, for everything in heaven and earth is yours. Yours, LORD, is the kingdom; you are exalted as head over all.

1 CHRONICLES 29:11

He is Lord of Lords, King of Kings, the highest Majesty, and Master of all things. Adonai is the plural of Adon, meaning "Lord, Master, or Owner." It has been translated "the One who possesses all things." He is master over all things—every possession, every behavior, every situation.

In Psalm 147:3–5, David says that the Lord "heals the brokenhearted and binds up their wounds. He determines the number of the stars and calls them each by name. Great is our Lord [*Adonai*] and mighty in power; his understanding has no limit." He is more powerful than we can imagine. And yet He is concerned about us.

There are many areas of life where we need God to rule as king—relationships, our thinking process, decision making. If there is an area that we have been keeping from God, it is up to us to ask Him in to guide and take charge. He is the owner of everything, the Master.

God is not too great to be concerned about our smallest wishes. He is not only King and Ruler of the universe, but also our Father in Christ Jesus.

Basilea Schlink

Adonai

We are not our own, any more than what we possess is our own. We did not make ourselves; we cannot be supreme over ourselves. We cannot be our own masters. We are God's property by creation, by redemption, by regeneration.

Cardinal John Henry Newman

Not of This World

Jesus said, "My kingdom is not of this world.... You say that I am a king. In fact, the reason I was born and came into the world is to testify to the truth. Everyone on the side of truth listens to me."

John 18:36–37

When the angel visited Mary to declare the arrival of Jesus through her He said, "He will be great and will be called the Son of the Most High. The Lord God will give him the throne of his father David, and He will reign over Jacob's descendants forever; his kingdom will never end" (Luke 1:32–33).

His kingdom is not of this world. It will never pass away, and we, because of Jesus, are part of it! When the great dragon, Satan, is finally defeated, a loud voice from heaven will shout, "Now have come the salvation and the power and the kingdom of our God, and the authority of his Messiah. For the accuser of our brothers and sisters, who accuses them before our God day and night, has been hurled down! They triumphed over him by the blood of the Lamb and by the word of their testimony" (Revelation 12:10–11).

As believers, followers of Jesus, we know the end of the story. Our Adonai, our Lord and King, will reign forever.

God is an inviting God. He invited Mary to birth His Son, the disciples to fish for men, the adulterous woman to start over, and Thomas to touch His wounds. God is the King who prepares the palace, sets the table, and invites His subjects to come in.

MAX LUCADO

Lord Master

Majesty

Therefore God exalted him to the highest place and gave him the name that is above every name, that at the name of Jesus every knee should bow, in heaven and on earth and under the earth, and every tongue acknowledge that Jesus Christ is Lord, to the glory of God the Father.

Philippians 2:9–11

Most people have not personally experienced the appearance of a president or king. But when given the chance to see one, people flock by the thousands, if not hundreds of thousands. The atmosphere is electric in anticipation of a mere glimpse of his or her majesty.

Take the most recent royal wedding, for example. Thousands of people lined the streets from the royal residence all the way to the church. Millions tuned in on television. They were all hoping to catch a glimpse of the future king and queen.

I once sang at a rally for the president of the United States. The crowd was pressing in from every side. They waited for hours. When the president made his appearance, the crowd erupted in praise and adoration. It took him several minutes to quiet them down enough for him to give his speech. Infinitely greater and more electrifying will it be when we see our King one day. For now we wait, watch, and hope.

We read His love letters to us in the Scriptures, we pray, we love, we sing, and one day soon, "We will see Him as He is" (1 John 3:2). All will bow, cheer, weep, and worship at the sound of His great name.

You already know that God is everywhere....
And where God is, there is heaven—heaven!
Where His Majesty reigns in glory.

St. Teresa of Avila

Adonai

Michael Neale, Dove Award–winning artist, songwriter, and master storyteller, is a sought after conference speaker, teacher, and concert artist. He impacts churches around the country as a seasoned communicator and performer. Author of the acclaimed novel *The River*, Michael also serves as artist-in-residence at Christ Fellowship in Palm Beach Gardens, Florida, where he lives with his wife, Leah, and their three children. For more information visit www.michaelneale.com.

In 2012, the song "Your Great Name" was named Worship Song of the Year at the Dove Awards.
